The Winter Olympics

The Winter Olympics

BY FRANK LITSKY

Franklin Watts
New York | London | Toronto | 1979
A First Book

OPPOSITE PAGE 1: THE OLYMPICS WERE
HELD TWICE IN INNSBRUCK—FIRST IN 1964
AND AGAIN IN 1976. IN 1976 THE DOUBLE
FLAME HERALDED THE OPENING OF THE
TWELFTH WINTER OLYMPICS.

Cover photograph courtesy of: Peter Arnold,
Inc.

Photographs courtesy of: *The New York
Times*: pp. 25, 42; Sygma: opp. p. 1; United
Press International: pp. 2, 11, 21, 27, 38, 41,
54, 59, 60, 62, 64, 65, 69; Wide World Photos:
pp. 6, 12, 16, 32, 45, 48, 51, 56, 63.

Library of Congress Cataloging in Publication Data

Litsky, Frank.
    The winter Olympics.

    (A First book)
    Bibliography: p.
    Includes index.
    SUMMARY: Explores the origins of the
Winter Olympics, recaps the games from 1924–
1976, and presents profiles of some of the athletes participating in these games.
    1. Olympic games (Winter)—History—Ju-
venile literature. 2. Athletes—Biography—Ju-
venile literature. [1. Olympic games (Winter)—
History. 2. Athletes] I. Title.
GV841.5.L55   796.9'8   79–10600
ISBN 0–531–02946–8

Contents

The Winter Olympics

The First Olympics

The original Olympic Games were first held in 776 B.C. in Olympia, near the west coast of Greece. At the beginning, there was only one event, a foot race the length of the stadium. Other running events and other sports were gradually added, and the Olympic Games became highly successful.

In time, winning became too important, and professionalism set in. Olympic champions, who were supposed to be pure amateurs, demanded and received huge rewards for winning. Things got so bad that the Romans, who then controlled that part of the world, abolished the Olympics in the fourth century A.D.

The Olympic Games were revived in 1896 through the efforts of Baron Pierre de Coubertin of France. They were held that year in Athens, Greece. Since then, summer games have been held every four years except for the war years of 1916, 1940 and 1944. They bring together the best athletes in the world in more than twenty sports. In some sports, Olympic competition establishes official world championships. The Games make a glittering spectacle that attracts spectators and television viewers worldwide.

[1]

The Olympic flag is carried out at the closing ceremonies
of the Winter Games in 1976. The American flag signifies
the 1980 Winter Games in Lake Placid, New York;
the Austrian flag flies for the host of the 1976 Games,
and the Greek flag honors the first Olympic Games.

Origin of the Winter Olympics

The skills of winter sports first developed out of necessity. People who lived where there was snow and ice had to get from one place to another, so they invented skis, skates and bobsleds. A museum in Stockholm, Sweden, displays skis that are 5,000 years old. Iron skates were used in Scotland as far back as 1572, and skates made of bone and then wood were used before that. A figure-skating club was formed in Scotland in 1642, and speed skating already existed then.

In most cases, formal competition in winter sports started in the last half of the nineteenth century. There was competitive speed skating in Britain in 1814. Ice hockey, derived from field hockey, was first played in 1855 in Kingston, Ontario, Canada. There was competitive skiing in 1860 in Norway; figure skating (waltzing on skates) in 1864 in Vienna, Austria; bobsledding in 1877 in Klosters, Switzerland.

But when the modern Olympic Games began, no one thought of including winter sports. Then came 1908, and figure skating was included in the Summer Olympics in London, England. Figure skating and ice hockey were added to the 1920 Summer Olympics in Antwerp, Belgium.

These additions were highly successful and some members of the International Olympic Committee (IOC) thought there should be a separate Winter Olympics. Norway and Sweden opposed it, fearing that a Winter Olympics would detract from their Nordic Games. Baron de Coubertin was against a Winter Olympics. He thought having two Olympics would menace Olympic unity.

Meanwhile, in connection with the 1924 Summer Olympics in Paris, the French organized an International Winter Sports Week that year in Chamonix. The IOC members who wanted a Winter Olympics thought this was an ideal place to begin, and they voted to call the Chamonix competition the Winter Olympic Games.

It was only an experiment. But things went so well that in 1925 the IOC voted to stage a Winter Olympics every four years, in the same year that the Summer Olympics were held—and except for the war years, the Winter Olympics have been staged ever since.

Who Runs the Olympics?

The International Olympic Committee (IOC) is in complete charge of the Olympic Games, winter and summer. The IOC decides where the games will be held, and establishes the rules for all the athletes. It requires that all athletes be amateurs, although in truth some earn large sums of money as a direct result of their athletic skills and reputations.

The IOC has eighty-nine members. No country may have more than two members, and some have none. The Committee chooses its own members, who then act as ambassadors of the Olympic Games to their countries rather than as representatives of their countries to the IOC.

Critics of the IOC have called it "a collection of old, rich men." There are no women members, though there is no rule barring women. In truth, many members are old and rich, but recently there has been a shift toward younger members.

Lord Killanin of Ireland was elected president of the IOC in 1972 at age fifty-eight. He succeeded Avery Brundage of Chicago, Illinois, who retired at age eighty-four.

The individual sports in both Summer and Winter Olympics are handled by the international federations of each sport, subject to the overall control of the IOC. Each country's Olympic team is chosen by its national Olympic committee.

The Winter Olympics begin in February, or late January. Like the summer games, they include elaborate ceremonies—opening and closing parades of athletes, pledges by athletes and officials. Olympic flames are lighted in Olympia, Greece, and carried to the country where the Games are to take place. The flame is kept burning in a stadium there until the closing ceremonies. Medals are awarded to the most successful athletes—gold medals for first place, silver for second, bronze for third.

The IOC has 133 member nations, but most do not have enough cold weather to allow for extensive winter sports. There have never been more than thirty-seven countries competing in a Winter Olympics, and only three countries—the United States, Britain, and Sweden—have taken part in every Winter Olympics.

The gold medal is displayed by Dorothy Hamill of the United States. She won the women's figure skating competition in the 1976 Winter Olympic Games.

[7]

Why the Olympic Games?

Through the years, the Olympic Games have been censured for many reasons. Costs have become astronomical. Some athletes spend all their time training, usually with financial help from their governments. Commercialism has often overshadowed idealism.

The International Olympic Committee has frequently been asked what purpose the Olympic Games serve in modern society. In its 1972 publication, "Olympism," the IOC defined the purposes of the Olympics. The Committee explained that the purpose of the Games was not to offer participants the opportunity to win a medal or beat a record, nor to entertain spectators. Nor was it to prove to politicians that one system of government is better than another. And above all the purpose of the Games was not to provide athletes a springboard for a professional career.

According to the IOC, the true purposes of the Games are:

■　To draw the world's attention to the fact that physical training and competitive sports develop the health, strength and character of young people.

■　To teach principles of loyal and sporting friendship, which should apply in other spheres of life as well.

■　To stimulate the fine arts.

■　To put emphasis on sports as games and distractions rather than as commercial business, and to show that the devotion applied to sports is an end in itself, not a means toward material gain.

The Winter Olympic Events

There are seven sports in the Winter Olympics—skiing, speed skating, figure skating, ice hockey, bobsledding, luge and biathlon. Dogsled racing was also included in 1932 and skeleton-sled racing (cresta) in 1928 and 1948. Demonstation sports have been held occasionally, also.

Here is a look at the present Olympic events.

■ Alpine Skiing——Three events (special slalom, giant slalom and downhill) for men and the same three for women. Alpine events were first held in the Olympics in 1936, and the present schedule was begun in 1948.

Ice dancing was added to the skating events in 1976. The Soviet pair, Ludmila Pakhomova and Aleksandr Gorshkov, won the gold medal. They are shown performing their first dance.

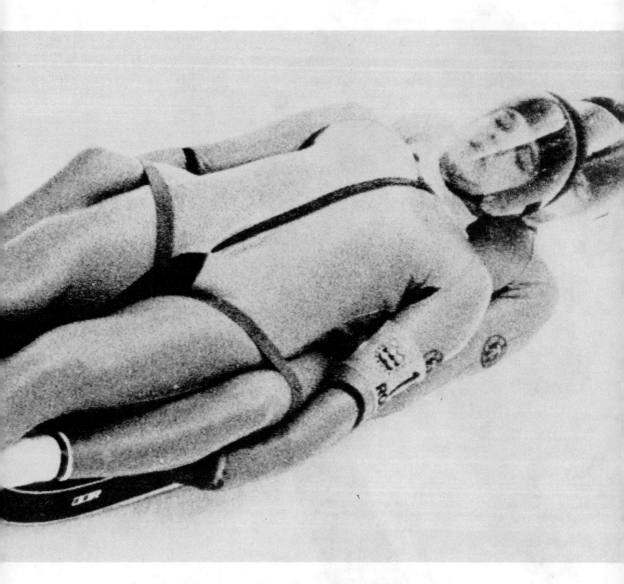

The luge sled, dashing through the chute, looks like a scene from science fiction.

■   Nordic Skiing——Seven events for men (four cross-country races, two jumping events and the "Nordic combined," which combines a cross-country race and a ski jump). There are three events for women (all cross-country races). The men have been included since 1924, the women since 1964.

■   Speed Skating——Five races for men and four for women. The athletes skate two at a time, and the winner is the skater with the best time overall. The men have been on the Olympic schedule since 1924, the women since 1960.

■   Figure Skating——One event for men, one for women and two for couples. (Each team in Pairs and each in Ice Dancing has one man and one woman.) Figure Skating was part of the 1908 and 1920 summer games and has been in the Olympics ever since.

■   Ice Hockey——Team competition for men. The sport has been part of the Olympics since the 1920 summer games.

■   Bobsledding——Competition for men on two-man and four-man sleds. Each sled races four times, with final standings based on total time. This has been an Olympic sport since 1924.

■   Luge——Two events for men and one for women on small sleds steered by ropes. Final standings are based on total time. The first Olympic luge races were held in 1964.

■   Biathlon——Three events for men. This combination of cross-country skiing and rifle marksmanship made its Olympic debut in 1960.

The Winter Olympic Games

1924: Chamonix, France

The first Winter Olympics, like all their successors, were held in a winter resort in the middle of winter. That should have insured good winter-sports weather—plenty of snow and cold. But in Chamonix, as in most host cities to follow, the weather generated some suspense.

The week before the competition began, there was so much rain that the ice rink turned into a lake. Then, when all seemed lost, a sudden frost froze the water and everything was fine.

Nordic and Alpine countries like the idea of putting their most popular sports into the Olympics, and they supported the Games enthusiastically. In all, sixteen nations sent teams to the small French town in the shadow of Mount Blanc in the Alps.

There were thirteen events in five sports—figure skating, speed skating, Nordic skiing, ice hockey and bobsledding. Women were represented in only one event—figure skating—but the best remembered athlete of these Games was a woman.

Rather, she was an eleven-year-old girl. Her name was Sonja Henie. A few weeks before the Olympics she had won the Norwegian figure-skating championship. That year, she finished last in the Olympics, but in later years she would win gold medals in three Olympics.

Norway won more medals (including four gold) than any other nation. An American, Charles Jewtraw of Lake Placid, New York, won a gold medal in the 500-m speed skating. The best speed skater was Clas Thunberg of Finland, who won three gold medals, one silver and one bronze. In 1928, almost thirty-five years old, he won two more gold medals.

Thorleif Haug of Norway won three gold medals and one bronze in Nordic skiing. Canada won the hockey championship, winning games by such scores as 30–0, 22–0, 33–0 and 19–2.

1928:
St. Moritz, Switzerland

By the time the second Winter Olympics were held, even their strongest opponents conceded that they were exciting competition. The Games at St. Moritz attracted twenty-five nations, and again Norway won more medals than any other country.

Sonja Henie of Norway, fifteen years old and already world champion, won the women's figure skating for her first Olympic gold medal. She also introduced a skating style that revolutionized

the sport. Before her day, figure skating was little more than waltzing on ice. Her style was more like ballet than waltzing, and the public was enchanted by it.

The men's figure skating champion for the third straight Olympics was Gillis Grafstrom of Sweden. His streak had started in 1920 at the Summer Olympics in Antwerp. He won in 1928, and in 1932, twelve years after his first gold medal, he won a silver medal.

The United States won two gold medals and a silver one. The American victories came in bobsledding events that are no longer in the Olympics. One was five-man bobsledding, the only time that event has been in the Olympics. The five men raced lying down rather than sitting. William Fiske of New York City drove the winning sled.

The other United States bobsledding victory was won in skeleton sledding. The winner was Jennison Heaton of New Haven, Connecticut, and the silver medalist was his brother, John R. Heaton. This event, introduced to the Olympics in 1928, took place only once again, in 1948.

The 10,000-m speed-skating race ended in confusion and controversy. The fastest time was posted by the American athlete, Irving Jaffee of New York City. But with a few contestants still to race, the ice thawed. After long discussion, the officials ruled it was "no race," that all performances would be discounted.

American officials were angry, saying that the remaining skaters should have been told to race despite the thaw. They argued long but unsuccessfully, and official Olympic records today

Nineteen-year-old Sonja Henie practicing in St. Moritz. She won her first gold medal in 1928 at the age of fifteen—and won again in 1932 and in 1936!

show that there was no winner of the race. However, several American books list Jaffee as the winner.

1932:
Lake Placid, New York

The Olympic Games were held in the United States for the first time in 1932—the summer games in Los Angeles, California, and the winter games in Lake Placid, New York.

Lake Placid was then a village of 4,000 in the Adirondack Mountains, a two hours' drive south of Montreal, Quebec, Canada. It was the oldest winter resort in the United States, and a site well suited for the Winter Olympics.

The organizers invited the sixty-five nations that belonged to the International Olympic Committee. Seventeen accepted—an encouraging response in view of the worldwide economic depression. The games were officially opened by the Governor of New York, Franklin D. Roosevelt, one year before he became President of the United States.

For the only time in Winter Olympic history, the United States led all other nations winning six gold medals in the fourteen events. The Americans collected all their gold medals in two sports, winning all four events in speed skating and both events in bobsledding.

John Shea, a twenty-one-year-old Dartmouth College sophomore from Lake Placid, took the oath on behalf of all the athletes during the opening ceremonies. Then he gave his hometown a treat by winning the gold medals in the 500-m and 1,500-m speed-skating races. Irving Jaffee, twenty-five, of New York City, had missed out on a gold medal in 1928 when a thaw led to controversial no-contest ruling in the 10,000-m race. This time he won the 5,000-m and 10,000-m titles.

There was controversy in the speed skating events this time, too. The previous Olympics had been conducted under European rules, whereby participants skated two at a time and final standings were based on their individual times. American rules provided for pack skating. Several contenders skated at one time in elimination heats, and the ones who came in ahead advanced to the finals. Time was unimportant.

International speed-skating officials decided to run these Olympic races under American rules. They thought it was a proper gesture toward the host country, and they wanted to see how pack racing would look. But the European skaters were unfamiliar with this style of racing and did not do well, and American rules were never used again in the Winter Olympics.

Bobsledding could have been disastrous for the United States. The Americans never had the opportunity to try out the sleds, which had been imported from Switzerland. The United States trials were abandoned because of warm weather, thaw and rain, and a committee had to pick the American competitors without trial.

The committee did a good job, however. The two-man bobsledding was won by J. Hubert Stevens of Lake Placid (driver) and his brother, Curtis Stevens (brakeman). The winning four-man sled was driven by William Fiske, of New York City, who steered the five-man sled to victory in 1928.

One rider on the four-man sled was Eddie Eagan, the 1920 light-heavyweight boxing champion in the Antwerp Olympics. He had never been on a sled before his arrival in Lake Placid, but he made history. He was the first athlete to win gold medals in both Summer and Winter Olympics.

The figure-skating star, as expected, was Sonja Henie of Norway, who won her second Olympic gold medal. She was only nineteen years old.

1936:
Garmisch-Partenkirchen, Germany

The Winter Olympics returned to Europe in 1936, and both the winter and summer games, were held in Germany. Many Americans wanted the United States to boycott the Games because of the oppressive treatment of Jews in Nazi Germany. American officials decided to compete, saying that politics should not interfere with sports.

Norway, which had dominated the Winter Olympics before 1932, won the greatest number of gold medals again. All told, Norway took seven gold, five silver, and three bronze medals. The best of the Norwegians were Sonja Henie in women's figure skating, Birger Ruud in skiing, and Ivar Ballangrud in speed skating.

Miss Henie, now twenty-three years old, won her third straight Olympic gold medal. A few months later, she turned professional and became even more famous for her ice shows and motion pictures.

The twenty-eight-year-old Ruud won the ski jump for the second consecutive Olympics as 150,000 spectators looked on. At that time, there was also a combined Alpine skiing event for men in which each athlete competed in a downhill race and a slalom.

**Is it a bird . . .? Is it a plane . . .?
No, it's Birger Ruud of Norway in his
victory leap at the 1936 Winter Games.**

The standing was determined by overall performance. Ruud won the downhill race of this event and placed fourth overall. His performance was astounding because ski jumping and downhill racing are different sports requiring different skills. It was as if Sonja Henie had won events not only in figure skating but also in speed skating.

Norway swept the four speed-skating races, and Ballangrud almost did it by himself. He won the 500-m, 5,000-m and 10,000-m, and he finished second in the 1,500-m.

The only United States gold medal was won by the two-man bobsledding team of Ivan Brown and Alan Washbond of Keene Valley, New York. If a gold medal were given for sportsmanship, the American bobsledders might have won that, too. The Americans lent their spare sleds to their rivals, when accidents left Belgium, the Netherlands, and Rumania without sleds.

The major controversy came in ice hockey. Canada, a strong contender, objected when Great Britain included two native Canadians (along with eleven British-born players) in its lineup. However, the move was legal under international rules—and it did make a difference in the outcome.

The British team won, and its star was Jimmy Foster, one of the Canadian natives. Foster, the goalie, allowed only three goals in seven games.

1948:
St. Moritz, Switzerland

World War II wiped out the Olympic Games, winter and summer, in 1940 and 1944. When the Games resumed in 1948, the winter competition returned to St. Moritz, which had been the host city in 1928.

This time, controversy started long before the opening ceremonies. The problem was the United States ice hockey team. In fact, there were two teams.

One was sent by the Amateur Athletic Union, which had always selected the United States teams. The other team was sent by the American Hockey Association (AHA), a group sponsored by owners of rinks and professional ice hockey teams.

The International Ice Hockey Federation supported the AHA team, and the AAU team had the blessing of the United States Olympic Committee. The day before the games began, the International Olympic Committee (IOC) met to try to resolve the problem. But because its members could not agree, and no existing rules fit the situation, the committee declared both teams out of the Olympics.

The Swiss, however, felt that an American ice hockey team would attract paying spectators. With the backing of the International Ice Hockey Federation, the Swiss said they would permit the AHA team to play. The IOC responded by dropping ice hockey as an event in these Olympics.

That should have settled the question, but then the IOC reversed itself and reinstated hockey as an official sport in these games. But it also ruled that the games played by the AHA team would not count in the standings, and declared that the AHA team would not receive medals even if it finished first, second, or third! As it turned out, there was no further problem because the AHA team played badly.

The dispute had caused difficulties for the United States Olympic Committee, however. Rink owners, who usually made major contributions to finance Olympic ice-hockey teams, held back their money, and until the last minute there was a possibility that the United States would send no ice-hockey team. The team it finally sent (the AAU team) never played, although it marched in the opening parade (whereas the AHA team did not).

There were other problems. Two large Olympic flags were stolen. Fortunately the Swiss had three. Several United States bobsleds were sabotaged, although the damage was found in time and did not affect performances. Speed skaters did not like the racing rules and seemed ready to strike.

The United States won three gold medals. Its winners were Gretchen Fraser of Vancouver, Washington, in women's slalom skiing; Dick Button of Englewood, New Jersey, in men's figure skating; and a four-man bobsled driven by Francis Tyler of Lake Placid, New York.

The twenty-eight-year-old Mrs. Fraser was the first starter in the slalom and made the fastest first run. She was about to start her second and final run when the telephone from the starting line to the finish line failed. She had to wait for 17 minutes. Another skier might have succumbed to the pressure, but with her pigtails flying, she made another strong run. She thus became the first American, male or female, to win an Olympic gold medal in skiing.

Button, an eighteen-year-old Harvard freshman, became the first American to win an Olympic figure-skating championship. The women's champion was Barbara Ann Scott, a twenty-year-old Canadian.

Sweden and Norway made the best overall performances. The Soviet Union had been accepted by the International Olympic Committee in 1947, but it sent observers rather than athletes.

Eighteen-year-old Dick Button was the first American ever to win the Olympic figure-skating championship.

Huge sums of money are required to finance Olympic teams today, but it was not always that way. The United States team in 1948 had no trainers. Instead, two masseurs—one for men and one for women—were hired in St. Moritz at a total cost of $300.

1952:
Oslo, Norway

At the 1952 Winter Olympics a nineteen-year-old American woman, Andrea Mead Lawrence, won two gold medals in women's skiing. (Her husband, David, was also on the United States ski team and finished 35th in the giant slalom.)

The first gold medal of the Games was awarded in the women's giant slalom, and Mrs. Lawrence won. In her next event, the down-hill, she fell twice and finished a disappointing 17th. Then came the final women's Alpine skiing event, the special slalom, in which the skiers must zigzag through a series of "gates," each consisting of two poles.

On her first slalom run, the tip of a ski caught a gate, and she went flying. By the time she regained stride, she had lost 3 seconds. When she finished the run, all seemed lost. But on the second of her two runs, she attacked the course like a mad woman. She finished the run 2 seconds faster than anyone else, an astounding margin in the slalom, and she won the gold medal by eight-tenths of a second.

**Andrea Mead Lawrence
won two gold medals in the 1952
Olympics: the women's giant
slalom, and the women's slalom.**

In all, four gold medals were won by American athletes: Andrea Lawrence in women's giant slalom and slalom; Ken Henry of Chicago, Illinois, in the 500-m speed skating; and Dick Button of Englewood, New Jersey, who repeated his 1948 triumph in men's figure skating. (Button was a student at Harvard Law School, and his professors allowed him to miss classes only if he would take his books with him and study when he wasn't skating.) Two silver medals were won for the United States by Stan Benham of Lake Placid, New York, who drove United States bobsleds in the two-man and four-man competition. Jeanette Altwegg of Great Britain won the gold medal in women's figure skating, and the biggest winner of the 1952 Winter Games was Hjalmar Andersen, a twenty-eight-year-old truck driver from Norway, who won three of the four gold medals in men's speed skating.

1956:
Cortina d'Ampezzo, Italy

Russian athletes, who had been performing all kinds of heroic deeds at home, finally made their Olympic debut in 1956. Soviet officials promised that their athletes would win more gold medals than anyone else, and they did.

The Russians won six of the twenty-four gold medals—three (out of four) in speed skating, two in Nordic skiing, and one in ice hockey. The United States ice-hockey team gained the silver medal after losing only one game—to the Russians.

The individual hero of the games was Anton (Toni) Sailer, a handsome, twenty-year-old Austrian from Kitzbuhel. He won all three Alpine skiing gold medals in runaways—the giant slalom by 6.2 seconds, the special slalom by 4 seconds, the downhill by 3.5

seconds. He was fast and daring, but, in the words of Zeno Colo of Italy, a 1952 Olympic champion, "He is gentle with the snow."

Few others were gentle with the snow, mainly because snow was scarce. Before the games, there was no snow, then heavy snow, then a thaw. There were more rocks and ice than snow, and a French official warned, "If it doesn't snow soon, the downhill ski competition will be a race to the death."

It did not turn out to be quite that bad, but many athletes were injured because of erratic surfaces. One was Tenley Albright, a twenty-year-old figure skater and premedical student from New-ton Centre, Massachusetts. During a pre-Olympic workout, she tripped over a hole in the ice and slashed her right ankle. Her father, a surgeon, flew to Italy to treat her.

Apparently he did a good job because Albright, the silver medalist in 1952, won the gold medal in figure skating this time. Hayes Alan Jenkins of Colorado Springs, Colorado, fourth in 1952, won the men's gold medal, the only other one for an American at Cortina. The United States overwhelmed the opposition in figure skating, finishing 1–2–3 among the men and 1–2 among the women.

1960:
Squaw Valley, California

Before 1960, the Winter Olympics had been held at established winter resorts. The 1960 Games were held in a remote place that few people had ever heard of.

Squaw Valley was an undeveloped area in the High Sierra Mountains in California, an hour's drive from Reno, Nevada. It was only 2 miles (3.22 km) long and ½ mile (.81 km) wide, and when

[29]

it was awarded the Olympics, it had only one ski lift and two rope tows.

The United States government, the states of California and Nevada and some private interests put up the $20,000,000 needed to build Olympic facilities. Construction was finished barely in time.

For the first part of the winter, there was no snow. Then, two weeks before the Olympics, it rained for 30 hours. Next came a 24-hour blizzard—and finally there was enough snow.

The opening pageant was staged by Walt Disney, and the cast included fifty-two school bands. Then came the competition, and again the major winner was the Soviet Union with seven gold medals (six in speed skating) in the twenty-seven events.

The United States won three gold medals, all on the ice. Two were in figure skating, as in 1956. David Jenkins of Colorado Springs, Colorado, won the men's competition and Carol Heiss of New York City won the women's. In 1956, Heiss gained a silver medal and Jenkins a bronze. Jenkins' brother, Hayes Alan Jenkins, was the 1956 champion, and later he married Carol Heiss.

The other American gold medal was won in ice hockey under dramatic circumstances. The Soviet Union and Canada were expected to excel, but the United States upset both and put the unbeaten Americans into the final game against Czechoslovakia. The Czechoslovaks were a national team. The United States team was a hastily-assembled group that included two carpenters, two insurance agents, a fireman, a soldier, and a television advertising salesman.

Czechoslovakia led, 4–3, after two periods, and the Americans were short of breath in the thin air at this high altitude. They were resting in their dressing room between the second and third periods when a visitor walked in. He was Nikolai Sologubov, a Russian army officer and captain of the Soviet Union's ice-hockey team.

Sologubov spoke no English. No American spoke Russian. But

using sign language, Sologubov got across his message. He told the Americans to inhale oxygen. They did, and they scored six goals in the last period and won the game, 9–4, and the gold medal. They had finished the Olympics undefeated.

In speed skating, the Russians had two double winners—Lidia Skoblikova among the women, and Yevgeni Grishin among the men. Grishin had also won two gold medals in 1956, although he considered himself better as a cyclist (he was a 1952 Olympic cyclist) than as a skater.

America's best skier was Penny Pitou of Laconia, New Hampshire, with two silver medals. In the downhill, after a near fall on a 90-degree corner, she was beaten by one second. Later, she said, "I think only willpower kept me up." In the giant slalom, hindered by a cold that affected her breathing, she lost by only one-tenth of a second.

1964:
Innsbruck, Austria

Innsbruck seemed a perfect setting for the Winter Olympics. As Arthur Daley wrote, "The main facilities there had been in place for at least a million years." But, as so often happens, the weather was treacherous.

Temperatures were high and there was little snow. Austrian soldiers had to deliver snow and ice in trucks. Then came rain, and courses became dangerous. A British tobogganer and an Australian skier were killed in pre-Olympic accidents, and many others were injured.

The competition again provided a display for Soviet athletes, who won eleven gold medals. Their stars were Lidia Skoblikova, who

[31]

swept the four women's gold medals in speed skating, and Claudia Boyarskikh, who swept the three women's gold medals in Nordic skiing. Skoblikova and Boyarskikh were twenty-four-year-old teachers from Siberia.

The only American gold medalist was twenty-three-year-old Terry McDermott of Essexville, Michigan, in the 500-m speed skating. The silver medalist was Yevgeni Grishin, the Russian who had won in 1956 and 1960.

The major upset was provided by the British two-man bobsled, which beat the favored Italians, and won the gold medal. The British driver was Antony (Tony) Nash, a manufacturer of light machinery, and the brakeman was Robin Dixon, a captain in the Grenadier Guards.

American men won their first Olympic skiing medals when Billy Kidd of Stowe, Vermont, finished second, and Jimmy Heuga of Tahoe City, California, third in the special slalom. Jean Saubert of Lakeview, Oregon, won a silver and a bronze medal in women's skiing.

The most successful women skiers were the Goitschel sisters of France. In the special slalom, nineteen-year-old Christine finished first, and eighteen-year-old Marielle, who had been expected to win, finished second. In the giant slalom, Marielle finished first and Christine tied for second.

The British two-man bobsled team in their second run down the chute at Innsbruck. The British shot out in front of the favored Italians with two record runs for a combined, leading time of 2:10.63.

1968:
Grenoble, France

The Winter Olympics held in 1968 at Grenoble were much more costly than previous Games. To start with, Grenoble was not a winter resort but a modern industrial city in the Alps. Some competition sites were up to 40 miles (64 km) from the city, and little Olympic Villages were built at these sites to house the athletes.

The total cost was $240,000,000, which included public buildings. A huge, open, horseshoe-shaped stadium to hold 60,000 to 70,000 spectators was built just for the opening ceremonies. Workmen started tearing it down the next day.

Fog, wind, and rain caused difficulties for athletes—especially American skiers. Eight of the American team of fourteen were injured during the Games.

Jean-Claude Killy, a twenty-four-year-old Frenchman, survived the weather to win all three Alpine events—downhill, special slalom, and giant slalom. Toni Sailer, who won all three in 1956, is the only other skier, male or female, who has achieved that sweep.

Despite Killy's heroic performance, Norway won the greatest number of gold medals, with the Soviet Union second. The United States took only one gold medal—in women's figure skating, where nineteen-year-old Peggy Fleming of Colorado Springs, Colorado, won easily.

The Americans caused a stir in the 500-m race of women's speed skating. There were three Americans in the race—sixteen-year-old Dianne Holum of Northbrook, Illinois; eighteen-year-old Jenny Fish of Strongville, Ohio; and twenty-year-old Mary Meyers of St. Paul, Minnesota. All finished in 46.3 seconds and tied for second place, and each received a silver medal.

[34]

In bobsledding, Eugenio Monti, probably the best athlete ever in the sport, won both gold medals for Italy. In luge, officials discovered that the steel runners of the East German women's toboggans had been heated to make the toboggans go faster, and the East Germans were disqualified. The International Luge Federation later reinstated them, saying there was no proof that the East Germans had committed the offense.

1972:
Sapporo, Japan

For the first time, the Winter Olympics were held in Asia. Sapporo is an industrial city on the most northern of the Japanese islands, the largest city ever to stage the winter games. The Japanese spent $31,000,000 for the Olympics—not counting $119,500,000 for a "silent" railway system running underground on rubber wheels that remained in use after the Olympics.

The Games were highly successful, but for a while it seemed they might never take place. The problem was commercialism among athletes, especially Alpine skiers.

Many European skiers were paid by manufacturers for displaying sports equipment: whenever a picture was taken, the athlete made sure that the manufacturer's name was visible on skis, boots, and bindings.

The International Ski Federation permitted this practice, but Avery Brundage, the crusty old president of the International Olympic Committee, said such commercialism violated Olympic rules. He said he had a list of forty skiers who had allowed their names and photographs to be used in advertising, and he wanted to bar them from competition. The ski federation threatened to boycott the Olympics if any skier was barred. The controversy raged for more than a year.

In the end, Brundage compromised. He barred one skier—Karl Schranz, a thirty-three-year-old Austrian who was expected to excel in all three Olympic events. Schranz was making $50,000 a year from manufacturers, and his sin might have been that he talked too much about it. So after fifteen years of world-class skiing, Schranz retired from the sport and flew home to a hero's welcome.

The United States took three gold medals, all won by women. Two gold medalists—twenty-year-old Dianne Holum and sixteen-year-old Anne Henning—were speed skaters from Northbrook, Illinois. This Chicago suburb of 27,000 had produced five of the seventeen women on the United States Olympic speed-skating team.

Holum, a silver medalist in 1968, won the 1,500-m race. Henning, a high-school junior, won the 500-m title, which she said was almost as exciting as playing halfback on her girls' intramural football team.

The other American winner was Barbara Ann Cochran of Richmond, Vermont, in the women's special slalom. The twenty-one-year-old Miss Cochran had her own cheering section—a sister and a brother on the Olympic team. She won the gold medal by two-hundredths of a second.

One American who excited the spectators was eighteen-year-old Janet Lynn of Rockford, Illinois, who finished third in women's figure skating. Although she lost ground in the compulsory figures, she electrified the crowd with her acrobatic, theatrical free skating, and took home the bronze medal.

The men's speed skating provided a triple gold medalist in

Adrianus (Ard) Schenk of the Netherlands. The tall, twenty-seven-year-old physiotherapist might have swept the board had he not stumbled and fallen at the start of the 500-m race.

In this Olympics, the Soviet Union led the way with sixteen medals—eight of them gold medals. The biggest Soviet winner was Galina Koulakova, who won three gold medals in women's cross-country skiing.

1976:
Innsbruck, Austria

The 1976 Winter Olympics were awarded at first to Denver, Colorado, in the heart of the Rocky Mountains. But in November 1972, Colorado voters rejected a bond issue to finance the Games. They did not want to be responsible for a large debt, and they feared that the environment would be spoiled.

The Games were not homeless for long. Innsbruck, Austria, which had played host in 1964, took them again. Costs had increased sharply and had scared off other potential host cities. But at Innsbruck, most of the facilities were already in place, and Innsbruck promised "simple games." The city spent $148,000,000, however, mostly on permanent facilities. It made up for some of that expense by charging $18 to $54 for tickets.

More money came from television. The American Broadcasting Company paid $10,000,000 for American television rights and spent $10,000,000 more in production costs. ABC took in $20,000,000 to $25,000,000 for advertising commercials.

The United States had three gold medalists—nineteen-year-old Dorothy Hamill of Riverside, Connecticut, in figure skating;

and twenty-five-year-old Sheila Young of Detroit, Michigan, and twenty-one-year-old Peter Mueller of Mequon, Wisconsin, in speed skating.

Hamill, who could have coasted to victory after building a huge lead, put on a sensational display of free skating. So did John Curry, a twenty-six-year-old from Great Britain, who won the men's figure skating with an elegant style borrowed from ballet. Both Hamill and Curry were coached by Carlo Fassi, an Italian who lived in Colorado Springs.

Sheila Young, a world champion in cycling and speed skating, won three speed skating medals in three days—gold in 500-m, silver in 1,500-m, and bronze in 1,000-m. Her success came despite speed skating's second-class status in the United States. In 1976, there was only one Olympic-sized (400-m) rink in the entire country—in West Allis, Wisconsin.

Mueller was so tense that he could not eat for two days before the 1,000-m race—but he won. His fiance, twenty-four-year-old Leah Poulos, won the silver medal in the women's 1,000-m, beaten by only four-hundredths of a second. Mueller and Poulos had used family savings to train in West Berlin, Germany, before the Olympics.

In Alpine skiing the heroine was Rosi Mittermaier, a twenty-five-year-old West German. She won gold medals in the women's downhill and special slalom, and a silver medal in the giant slalom.

The first gold medal of the games was awarded in the men's downhill. The competitor expected to win was twenty-two-year-old Franz Klammer of Austria, and there was great pressure on him.

**Peter Mueller of Wisconsin
takes the gold medal in
1,000-m speed-skating in 1976.**

He had carried the Austrian flag in the opening parade. He had taken the Olympic oath on behalf of all the athletes. Austria made it clear that tourism and national prestige were at stake.

Klammer felt that he had to win. And he did, with a breakneck style that put him constantly on the edge of disaster. As it turned out, he was the only Austrian gold medalist; the Austrian ski team, which had been expected to dominate the Games, won only two of the eighteen medals.

Bill Koch (pronounced Coke), an American from Guilford, Vermont, provided a surprise in Nordic skiing. Despite asthma that restricted his breathing, the twenty-year-old Koch won the silver medal in the 30-km race, only 29 seconds behind the winner. The best previous achievement by an American in Olympic Nordic skiing had been a 15th place forty-four years before. Koch relished the moment, saying, "This will forever be the most beautiful day in my life."

Right: icy conditions make the downhill run very dangerous. This is Austria's Franz Klammer, 1976 gold-medal winner on the treacherous Patscherkofel course.

Over: an Olympic ski-jumper against a backdrop of Tyrolean Alps at the 1976 Winter Games.

The Great Athletes

SONJA HENIE,
the Norwegian Doll

The most famous of all Winter Olympic athletes may have been Sonja Henie (pronounced SOWN-yah HEN-knee), a figure skater from Norway.

When she started, figure skating was a sport for people in northern countries, where ice was plentiful outdoors. In other countries, only the rich skated. When she left the sport, there were artificial ice rinks everywhere.

Henie made her Olympic debut in 1924, the first year of the Winter Olympics. She was only eleven years old, and she finished last, but she went on to win the gold medals in 1928, 1932, and 1936. Then she turned professional and formed the first ice show. In addition to her three Olympic gold medals, Sonja Henie had won ten straight world championships, eight straight European championships, and six straight Norwegian championships.

[43]

She starred in eleven motion pictures. She was not a good actress, but she skated in every picture, and all her pictures made money. Her skating and acting career earned her $47,000,000.

Henie's impact on figure skating was great. Before her day, free skating was a series of figures and stunts unrelated to one another. There was no flow and no unity. Sonja had studied ballet, and she made it a part of her free skating. In her ice shows, she also did the Charleston, hula and other dances on skates.

As a later champion, Dick Button, said, "She clearly affected the sport more than anyone before and after." And as Carlo Fassi, a modern-day coach, said, "She brought skating to the world."

DICK BUTTON, the Athletic Skater

The best male figure skater in history was Dick Button. His technique was so good and so smooth that he made the difficult look simple. His coach, Gus Lussi, said he was perfect to work with because, "nothing short of perfection will satisfy him."

His career did not start well, however. When Dick was twelve years old, his parents asked a club professional to coach him. The coach watched the 5-foot-2-inch (1.57-m), 160-pound (72.5-kg) boy skate, then turned down the job.

"He'll never make a skater," said the coach. "Never. Not in a million years. He's too fat, for one thing. And he lacks coordination."

Dick found another coach and lost weight. And, despite what the club pro had said, Dick became a skater. At sixteen, he won the

Dick Button—nothing short of perfection would satisfy him.

first of seven straight United States figure-skating championships. At eighteen, he won the first of five straight world championships, and skated in the 1948 Olympics. When Dick was skating, his parents were nervous. His father was so tense during the Olympics that he dropped his cigar. But Dick was cool. He dazzled the judges with the jumps and spins he had invented, and he became the first American to win an Olympic figure-skating championship.

In 1952, he won the Olympic gold medal again. Then he retired as an amateur skater. He starred in the Ice Capades and later in his own ice show. He became a lawyer, businessman, and television packager—and an expert television commentator at skating events.

Dick Button introduced a new athletic style to figure skating. And he left with it a legacy of honesty that serves any sport and anything in life.

When he almost fell in the 1952 Olympics, Dick was asked if the ice was bad.

"The ice is never bad," he said. "Only the skater is bad."

TERRY McDERMOTT, the Skating Barber

In recent years, American speed skaters have done well in the Winter Olympics. But when Terry McDermott was skating, Americans won few medals because they did not train as hard as they do now.

Richard Terrance (Terry) McDermott started skating at the age of seven. His brother-in-law, a speed skating coach, put skates on him and carried him onto the ice. A year later, Terry won the Michigan cradle-division championship, and his career had started.

In 1960, Terry finished seventh in the Olympic 500-m race. In 1964, he tried again. He was 5 feet 9¼ inches (1.76 m) and 170 pounds (77 kg), solid and strong. But like most American skaters, he had prepared almost casually. While the Russians skated almost year round, Terry worked out only three hours a week for one month, then two hours a day for another month before the Games.

That seemed hardly enough, and few people thought Terry had a chance. He was even wearing skates borrowed from his coach. But when the race came, Terry bent far forward, skating with great power. He won the gold medal.

Then he went back home to Essexville, Michigan, and back to work in Bunny's Barber Shop in nearby Bay City. Bunny was Terry's uncle, and he had taught Terry to be a barber.

Terry retired from skating for two years. Then he came out of retirement, made the 1968 Olympic team and finished second in the 500-m race, beaten by only two-tenths of a second. Then he retired again—this time for good.

PEGGY FLEMING,
Ballerina on Ice

If Dick Button is the best male figure skater ever, Peggy Fleming may be the best female figure skater. Just as Button made a major contribution with his athletic style, Peggy Fleming made one with her slow, tender, ballet style.

One onlooker described her style by saying, "She floats across life like a prima ballerina."

Peggy was born in San Jose, California. Her father was a newspaper pressman and moved from job to job. He finally moved to Colorado Springs, Colorado, so Peggy could get the best coaching.

In 1964, at the age of fifteen, she won the first of five straight United States championships. Then she went to the Winter Olympics and finished sixth, which should have made her proud. But when she returned to high school, her classmates said only, "You didn't win a medal." Peggy said later, "I was crushed, but I think I really grew up as a result."

In 1968, when she was world champion, she skated in the Olympics again. This time, she was the star. With the world watching on live television, she skated as in a dream. At 105 pounds (47.5 kg), slim and delicate, she looked like a ballerina and skated like one. She won the gold medal with the highest scores in Olympic history.

Then she signed a $500,000 contract to skate in ice shows and do television specials. Ten years later, a wife and mother, she was still skating in ice shows and still loving every moment.

JEAN-CLAUDE KILLY,
the French Flier

He was almost too good to be true. He was robust, handsome, and charming. His smile lighted up his face. And he was the best Alpine skier of his day. But Olympic success did not come easily for Jean-Claude Killy of France.

He started skiing at the age of three in the French Alps, where he lived, and he became the best. But the pressure was fierce in the 1968 Winter Olympics.

Peggy Fleming won the gold medal in 1968 with the highest scores in Olympic history.

[49]

To start with, the Olympics were in France that year, and everyone there expected Killy to win every race and told him so. Just before the games, Killy had all kinds of racing problems, losing two downhills and falling twice in slaloms. Then, after the games had started, Avery Brundage, president of the International Olympic Committee, again charged that commercialism had taken over skiing. For a while, it looked as if Brundage would cancel the Olympic skiing races.

Then the controversy simmered down, and Killy went to work. First, he won the downhill by only eight-hundredths of a second. Then he won the giant slalom easily. Only the special slalom remained.

The race started in heavy fog. Killy did well, and only Karl Schranz of Austria stood between him and a third gold medal.

Schranz, charging down the snow on the second of his two runs, stopped after the 22nd gate. He said a course guard, whose job was to keep spectators from wandering onto the course, had wandered onto the course himself, right in Schranz' path. Two officials and one opponent confirmed the story, and Schranz was allowed another run. He did so well on it that he posted the fastest time. The gold medal seemed to be his.

But not for long. The course had been lined with officials who made sure each skier went through each gate. The official responsible for one set of gates reported that, on his original second run, Schranz had missed two gates before he was interfered with. So the rerun of his second run should not have been allowed, and it was wiped out. Schranz was disqualified, and Killy won his third gold medal. "Now," he said, "I am on the summit."

Killy retired later that year because, he said, "What else is there for me to win?" He did television commercials and made appearances, and later he had a short but successful career as a professional skier.

**Jean-Claude Killy flies through the gates
in the 1968 Olympic giant slalom.**

EUGENIO MONTI,
King of Bobsledding

Eugenio Monti of Italy wanted to be an Alpine skier. Instead, he became the most celebrated bobsledder in history.

He was on his way to becoming one of Italy's best skiers until a severe spill in 1952. He tore ligaments in both knees and underwent surgery, but he was finished as a skier. When he recovered from surgery, he drove sports cars, and then, in 1954, he turned to bobsledding.

Until then, bobsledders had been huge men on the theory that the heavier the men on the sled, the faster the sled would go. Monti was only 5 feet 9 inches (1.75 m) and 145 (66 kg) pounds, but his skill more than made up for his lack of size.

In 1956, in the Winter Olympics in his home town of Cortina d'Ampezzo, Italy, Monti won two silver medals. There was no Olympic bobsledding in 1960. In 1964, he won two bronze medals. In 1968, with nine world championships behind him, he made his last stand in the Olympics.

Monti won the four-man title by nine-hundredths of a second for the four runs. In the two-man competition, he and the Germans had the identical time to the hundredth of a second. Ties were broken on the fastest single run, and Monti had the fastest by a tenth of a second. So Monti won his two gold medals and became the oldest medalist of those games. Then he retired, saying:

"Now I can stop. At forty, it is too old for the bobsled."

Monti was a true sportsman. In the 1964 Olympics, just before the British sled was to make its second run, Monti heard an announcement that a bolt supporting the runners had broken off the sled. Monti took the bolt off his own sled, hurried up the hill and repaired the British sled himself. The British sled went on to win the gold medal.

For his unselfish deed, Monti became, in 1965, the first recipient of the Pierre de Coubertin Fair Play Trophy. He was nominated by Antony (Tony) Nash, the driver of the British sled.

DOROTHY HAMILL,
Short and Sassy

The most attractive event in the Winter Olympics may be the free skating portion of women's figure skating. This is the stage for the daring leaps and spins and jumps that make figure skating so enjoyable. No one in modern times has made it more enjoyable than Dorothy Hamill, the 1976 Olympic champion.

Dorothy was eight years old when her mother and father gave her ice skates for Christmas. She started skating on a frozen pond near her home in Riverside, Connecticut. Soon she asked for lessons, and at age fourteen she dropped out of school and studied with a tutor so she could have enough time to work out. Later, she left home and moved to Colorado Springs, Colorado, to train seven hours a day, six days a week, eleven months a year.

It paid off when she became Olympic champion at age nineteen. She was a popular champion—graceful, modest, and charming, and she had a beautiful smile. She knew what the public and the judges wanted and she had the skill to provide it. A perfect score in figure skating is 6. Every Olympic judge gave her 5.9 for the free-skating performance.

By the end of the 1976 season, she held the Olympic, world, and United States championships. Then she retired from amateur

skating, joined the Ice Capades and performed all over the country. She also appeared on television shows and advertising commercials. Her hairstyle was widely imitated and even people who had never heard of figure skating got to know her when she talked about hair products that provided the short and sassy look.

JOHN CURRY,
the Elegant Skater

When Dick Button became Olympic figure-skating champion in 1948, he introduced an athletic style that the best skaters used for almost thirty years. When John Curry of Great Britain won the gold medal in 1976, he did it with an elegant style. The emphasis of his routine was on ballet rather than athletic skill.

When John was six years old, he wanted to become a dancer, but his father opposed it. When John was seven, he went skating for the first time—and he loved it. He took lessons and improved rapidly, although he didn't like the jumping part of free skating.

In 1972, he placed fourth in the world championships. In 1973, he finished seventh and became discouraged. He wanted to quit. But an American patron gave him money to move to the United States. There John resolved to modify his style and learn to jump well, and in 1976, at twenty-six, he won the Olympic, world, and European titles. Then he turned professional, but instead of joining a conventional ice show, he formed his own troupe and commissioned choreographers to prepare his routines.

Nineteen-year-old Dorothy Hamill.
In 1976 she held Olympic,
world, and U.S. championships.

[55]

His skating style remained controversial. A West German judge had once criticized him by saying his skating style was not "manly" enough. Curry answered by saying: "I threaten them, I guess. It's so ridiculous, as if someone had to skate in a little soldier way to win a gold medal. Skating should be beautiful. It's lost some of its elegance."

If so, John Curry restored elegance to the sport.

SHEILA YOUNG, Two-Sport Champion

On the surface, speed skating and bicycle racing seem far apart. But the key to both sports is strong thigh muscles, and athletes who are good in one sport may be good in the other, too.

The prime example is Sheila Young. Although she never raced bicycles in the Summer Olympics, she won the world sprint title in bicycle racing in 1973 and again in 1976. In speed skating, she won many world titles, and she won three Olympic medals in three days in 1976.

Sheila's mother and father were cycling champions, and her brother, Roger, became a Pan-American Games champion. Sheila learned cycling and speed skating when she was young. When Sheila was thirteen, her mother died, and her father cared for the children alone. So when he took one child skating, they all went skating.

John Curry's brilliant freestyle performance won Britain's first gold medal in men's figure skating.

In the 1972 Winter Olympics, Sheila just missed winning a medal, finishing fourth in the 500-m race. She thought about quitting, but instead she trained harder than ever.

She worked out four hours a day. She trained by skating six months of the year and by running the other six months. And she covered long distances in a crouch, looking like Groucho Marx on the run. That helped build up the thighs.

Sheila wanted her fiancé, Jim Ochowicz, to watch her in the 1976 Olympics. They had no money. So she sold her racing bike for $250 to buy a plane ticket for Jim, and they went to Innsbruck. Every morning there, they ran together. Jim was able to keep up because he was in good condition. He was a cyclist, too.

Sheila was top contender in the Olympic 500-m race, but she had a strained ligament in the left foot and had to bandage it tightly each morning. "I'll try to skate my best," she said, and she did, winning the gold medal. She earned the silver medal at 1,500-m and the bronze at 1,000-m.

After the 1976 Olympics, Sheila and Jim were married. In December 1977, they had their first child, a daughter named Katie. Their new home was Lake Placid, New York, where Sheila and Jim worked for the committee planning the 1980 Winter Olympics there.

ROSI MITTERMAIER, "Grandma on Skis"

When Rosi Mittermaier of West Germany was sixteen years old, she was already competing in World Cup ski races. For nine years, she

Sheila Young, of Detroit, Michigan, won three speed-skating medals in three days at the 1976 Olympics.

raced, seldom winning the big events. She was a fine skier technically, but something always happened. She seemed to lack concentration, and she had bad luck, too. In Hawaii, taking a vacation from skiing, she was struck by a surfboard. On the ski slopes, a ski tourist crashed into her.

But Rosi never gave up. She was always bubbly, a happy, friendly person. Sooner or later, her day would come.

It came in the 1976 Olympics. First, she won the women's downhill in an upset. Three days later, she won the special slalom. She was so popular among her fellow athletes that when she walked into the athletes' dining room that night she got a standing ovation.

Two days after the special slalom came the giant slalom, and Rosi's try for a third Olympic medal. Almost everyone was rooting for her.

Kathy Kreiner of Canada, who had never won a major race, won the gold by twelve-hundredths of a second over Rosi. But Rosi took the silver, managing to stay on her feet after hitting two control gates toward the end of the run. Her collection of two gold medals and one silver one was the best performance by a woman Alpine skier in Winter Olympic history.

After the Olympics, Rosi won the World Cup series championship and then retired from skiing at age twenty-five.

"They have already dubbed me the grandma on skis," she said. "I would prefer that they didn't start calling me the great-grandmother."

**West Germany's Rosi Mittermaier
on her way to a second gold medal.
This is the women's slalom, 1976.**

The streamlined outfits and stretch fabric
of today make an amusing contrast to the
awkward, baggy clothing of earlier times.
Compare Dorothy Hamill (*left*) in 1976
with Sonja Henie (*above*) in 1928.

Olympic athletes are models of endurance and daring. Here are Bill Koch of the United States (*above*) and Hans-Georg Aschenbach of East Germany (*left*).

The Winter Olympics: Where and When

		NATIONS PARTICIPATING
1924	Chamonix, France	16
1928	St. Moritz, Switzerland	25
1932	Lake Placid, New York, U.S.A.	17
1936	Garmisch-Partenkirchen, Germany	28
1940	Not held	
1944	Not held	
1948	St. Moritz, Switzerland	28
1952	Oslo, Norway	30
1956	Cortina d'Ampezzo, Italy	32
1960	Squaw Valley, California, U.S.A.	30
1964	Innsbruck, Austria	36
1968	Grenoble, France	37
1972	Sapporo, Japan	35
1976	Innsbruck, Austria	37

Winter Olympic Medals, 1924–1976

	GOLD	SILVER	BRONZE	TOTAL
Norway	49	51	42	142
U.S.S.R.	49	34	35	118
United States	30	40	27	97
Austria	22	31	27	80
Finland	23	34	21	78
Sweden	22	21	25	68
Switzerland	15	17	16	48
East Germany	12	10	16	38
*Germany	14	11	10	35
France	12	9	12	33
Canada	11	7	14	32
The Netherlands	9	10	9	28
Italy	10	7	7	24
West Germany	7	8	7	22

*Competed as one team until 1964

Great Britain	4	2	6	12
Czechoslovakia	2	5	5	12
Hungary	0	1	4	5
Japan	1	2	1	4
Belgium	1	1	2	4
Poland	1	1	2	4
Liechtenstein	0	0	2	2
Spain	1	0	0	1
North Korea	0	1	0	1
Rumania	0	0	1	1

Opposite: jubilant British ice hockey players after winning the gold medal at Garmish Partenkirchen, Germany, in the 1936 Winter Olympics.

Winter Olympic Champions

ALPINE SKIING

MEN'S DOWNHILL

1948 Henri Oreiller, France
1952 Zeno Colo, Italy
1956 Toni Sailer, Austria
1960 Jean Vuarnet, France
1964 Egon Zimmermann, Austria
1968 Jean-Claude Killy, France
1972 Bernhard Russi, Switzerland
1976 Franz Klammer, Austria

MEN'S GIANT SLALOM

1952 Stein Eriksen, Norway
1956 Toni Sailer, Austria
1960 Roger Staub, Switzerland
1964 François Bonlieu, France
1968 Jean-Claude Killy, France
1972 Gustavo Thoeni, Italy
1976 Heini Hemmi, Switzerland

WOMEN'S DOWNHILL

1948 Hedi Schlunegger, Switzerland
1952 Trude Jochum-Beiser, Austria
1956 Madeleine Berthod, Switzerland
1960 Heidi Biebl, Germany
1964 Christl Haas, Austria
1968 Olga Pall, Austria
1972 Marie-Therese Nadig, Switzerland
1976 Rosi Mittermaier, West Germany

WOMEN'S GIANT SLALOM

1952 Andrea Mead Lawrence, United States
1956 Ossi Reichert, Germany
1960 Yvonne Ruegg, Switzerland
1964 Marielle Goitschel, France
1968 Nancy Greene, Canada
1972 Marie-Therese Nadig, Switzerland
1976 Kathy Kreiner, Canada

ALPINE SKIING
(continued)

MEN'S SLALOM

1948 Edi Reinalter, Switzerland
1952 Othmar Schneider, Austria
1956 Toni Sailer, Austria
1960 Ernst Hinterseer, Austria
1964 Pepi Stiegler, Austria
1968 Jean-Claude Killy, France
1972 Francisco Fernandez Ochoa, Spain
1976 Piero Gros, Italy

WOMEN'S SLALOM

1948 Gretchen Fraser, United States
1952 Andrea Mead Lawrence, United States
1956 Renee Colliard, Switzerland
1960 Anne Heggtveit, Canada
1964 Christine Goitschel, France
1968 Marielle Goitschel, France
1972 Barbara Cochran, United States
1976 Rosi Mittermaier, West Germany

BIATHLON
(Skiing and Shooting)

20-KM

		HR.-MIN.-SEC.
1960	Klas Lestander, Sweden	1:33:21.6
1964	Vladimir Melanin, U.S.S.R.	1:20:26.8
1968	Magnar Solberg, Norway	1:13:45.9
1972	Magnar Solberg, Norway	1:15:55.50
1976	Nikolai Kruglov, U.S.S.R.	1:14:12.26

40-KM RELAY

		HR.-MIN.-SEC.
1968	U.S.S.R.	2:13:02.4
1972	U.S.S.R.	1:51:44.92
1976	U.S.S.R.	1:57:55.64

BOBSLEDDING

TWO-MAN

		MIN.-SEC.
1932	U.S. (Hubert Stevens)	8:14.74
1936	U.S. (Ivan Brown)	5:29.29
1948	Switzerland (Felix Endrich)	5:29.2
1952	Germany (Andreas Ostler)	5:24.54
1956	Italy (Dalla Costa)	5:30.14
1960	Not held	
1964	Great Britain (Antony Nash)	4:21.90
1968	Italy (Eugenio Monti)	4:41.54
1972	West Germany (Wolfgang Zimmerer)	4:57.07
1976	East Germany (Meinhard Nehmer)	3:44.42

Driver indicated in parentheses

FOUR-MAN

		MIN.-SEC.
1924	Switzerland (Edward Scherrer)	5:45.54
1928	U.S. (William Fiske)	3:20.5 *
1932	U.S. (William Fiske)	7:53.68
1936	Switzerland (Pierre Musy)	5:19.85
1948	U.S. (Edward Rimkus)	5:20.1
1952	Germany (Andreas Ostler)	5:07.84
1956	Switzerland (Franz Kapus)	5:10.44
1960	Not held	
1964	Canada (Victor Emery)	4:14.46
1968	Italy (Eugenio Monti)	2:17.39†
1972	Switzerland (Jean Wicki)	4:43.07
1976	East Germany (Meinhard Nehmer)	3:40.43

*Five men on sled.
†Two races instead of four.

FIGURE SKATING

MEN'S SINGLES

1908 Ulrich Salchow, Sweden
1920 Gillis Grafstrom, Sweden
1924 Gillis Grafstrom, Sweden
1928 Gillis Grafstrom, Sweden
1932 Karl Schaefer, Austria
1936 Karl Schaefer, Austria
1948 Dick Button, United States
1952 Dick Button, United States
1956 Hayes Alan Jenkins, United States
1960 David Jenkins, United States
1964 Manfred Schnelldorfer, Germany
1968 Wolfgang Schwarz, Austria
1972 Ondrej Nepela, Czechoslovakia
1976 John Curry, Great Britain

WOMEN'S SINGLES

1908 Madge Syers, Great Britain
1920 Magda Julin-Mauroy, Sweden
1924 Herma Planck-Szabo, Austria
1928 Sonja Henie, Norway
1932 Sonja Henie, Norway
1936 Sonja Henie, Norway
1948 Barbara Ann Scott, Canada
1952 Jeanette Altwegg, Great Britain
1956 Tenley Albright, United States
1960 Carol Heiss, United States
1964 Sjoukje Dijkstra, Netherlands
1968 Peggy Fleming, United States
1972 Beatrix Schuba, Austria
1976 Dorothy Hamill, United States

FIGURE SKATING
(continued)

PAIRS

1908 Anna Hubler and Heinrich Burger, Germany
1920 Ludovika and Walter Jakobsson, Finland
1924 Helene Engelmann and Alfred Berger, Austria
1928 Andree Joly and Pierre Brunet, France
1932 Andree and Pierre Brunet, France
1936 Maxie Herber and Ernst Baier, Germany
1948 Micheline Lannoy and Pierre Baugniet,
     Belgium
1952 Ria and Paul Falk, Germany
1956 Elizabeth Schwarz and Kurt Oppelt, Austria
1960 Barbara Wagner and Robert Paul, Canada
1964 Ludmilla Belousova and Oleg Protopopov,
     U.S.S.R

1968 Ludmilla Belousova and Oleg Protopopov,
     U.S.S.R
1972 Irina Rodnina and Aleksei Ulanov,
     U.S.S.R.
1976 Irina Rodnina and Aleksandr Zaitsev,
     U.S.S.R.

ICE DANCING

1976 Ludmilla Pakhomova and
     Aleksandr Gorshkov, U.S.S.R.

ICE HOCKEY

1920 Canada
1924 Canada
1928 Canada
1932 Canada
1936 Great Britain
1948 Canada
1952 Canada
1956 U.S.S.R.
1960 United States
1964 U.S.S.R.
1968 U.S.S.R.
1972 U.S.S.R.
1976 U.S.S.R.

LUGE
(Tobogganing)

MEN'S SINGLES

1964 Thomas Koehler, Germany
1968 Manfred Schmid, Austria
1972 Wolfgang Scheidel, East Germany
1976 Detlef Guenther, East Germany

MEN'S DOUBLES

1964 Austria (Josef Pfiestmantl)
1968 East Germany (Klaus Bonsack)
1972 Tie between Italy (Paul Hildgartner)
     and East Germany (Horst Hornlein)
1976 East Germany (Hans Rinn)
     Driver indicated in parentheses

WOMEN'S SINGLES

1964 Ortrun Enderlein, Germany
1968 Erika Lechner, Italy
1972 Anna Maria Muller, East Germany
1976 Margit Schumann, East Germany

NORDIC SKIING

MEN'S 15-KM CROSS-COUNTRY

		HR.-MIN.-SEC.
1924	Thorlief Haug, Norway	1:14:31.0*
1928	Johan Grottumsbraaten, Norway	1:37:01.0†
1932	Sven Utterstrom, Sweden	1:23:07.0**
1936	Erik-August Larsson, Sweden	1:14:38.0*
1948	Martin Lundstroem, Sweden	1:13:50.0*
1952	Hallgein Brenden, Norway	1:01:34.0*
1956	Hallgein Brenden, Norway	49:39.0
1960	Haakon Brusveen, Norway	51:55.5
1964	Eero Maentyranta, Finland	50:54.1
1968	Harald Groenningen, Norway	47:54.2
1972	Sven-Ake Lundback, Sweden	45:28.24
1976	Nikolai Bashukov, U.S.S.R.	43:58.47

*18 km
†19,700 m
**18,214 m

MEN'S 30-KM CROSS-COUNTRY

		HR.-MIN.-SEC.
1956	Veikko Hakulinen, Finland	1:44:06.0
1960	Sixten Jernberg, Sweden	1:51:03.9
1964	Eero Maentyranta, Finland	1:30:50.7
1968	Franco Nones, Italy	1:35:39.2
1972	Vyacheslav Vedenin, U.S.S.R.	1:36:31.15
1976	Sergei Saveliev, U.S.S.R.	1:30:29.38

NORDIC SKIING
(continued)

MEN'S 50-KM
CROSS-COUNTRY

		HR.-MIN.-SEC.
1924	Thorlief Haug, Norway	3:44:32.0
1928	Per Erik Hedlund, Sweden	4:52:03.0
1932	Veli Saarinen, Finland	4:28:00.0*
1936	Elis Viklund, Sweden	3:30:11.0
1948	Nils Karlsson, Sweden	3:47:48.0
1952	Veikko Hakulinen, Finland	3:33:33.0
1956	Sixten Jernberg, Sweden	2:50:27.0
1960	Kalevi Hamalainen, Finland	2:59:06.3
1964	Sixten Jernberg, Sweden	2:43:52.6
1968	Ole Ellefsaeter, Norway	2:28:45.8
1972	Paal Tyldum, Norway	2:43:14.75
1976	Ivar Formo, Norway	2:37:30.05

*48,238 m

MEN'S 40-KM
CROSS-COUNTRY RELAY

		HR.-MIN.-SEC.
1936	Finland	2:41:33.0
1948	Sweden	2:32:08.0
1952	Finland	2:20:16.0
1956	U.S.S.R.	2:15:30.0
1960	Finland	2:18:45.6
1964	Sweden	2:18:34.6
1968	Norway	2:08:33.5
1972	U.S.S.R.	2:04:47.94
1976	Finland	2:07:59.72

NORDIC SKIING (continued)

MEN'S NORDIC COMBINED (CROSS-COUNTRY AND SKI JUMP)

		PTS.
1924	Thorleif Haug, Norway	453.800
1928	Johan Grottumsbraaten, Norway	427.800
1932	Johan Grottumsbraaten, Norway	446.200
1936	Oddbjorn Hagen, Norway	430.300
1948	Heikki Hasu, Finland	448.800
1952	Simon Slattvik, Norway	451.621
1956	Sverre Stenersen, Norway	455.000
1960	Georg Thoma, Germany	457.952
1964	Tormod Knutsen, Norway	469.280
1968	Franz Keller, West Germany	449.040
1972	Ulrich Wehling, East Germany	413.340
1976	Ulrich Wehling, East Germany	423.390

MEN'S 70-M JUMPING

		PTS.
1964	Veikko Kakkonen, Finland	229.9
1968	Jiri Raska, Czechoslovakia	216.5
1972	Yukio Kasaya, Japan	244.2
1976	Hans-Georg Aschenbach, East Germany	252.0

MEN'S 90-M JUMPING

		PTS.
1924	Jacob Thams, Norway	227.5
1928	Alfred Andersen, Norway	230.5
1932	Birger Ruud, Norway	228.0
1936	Birger Ruud, Norway	232.0
1948	Petter Hugsted, Norway	232.0
1952	Arnfinn Bergmann, Norway	226.0
1956	Antti Hyvarinen, Finland	227.0
1960	Helmut Recknagel, Germany	227.2
1964	Alf Engan, Norway	230.7
1968	Vladimir Beloussov, U.S.S.R.	231.3
1972	Wojciech Fortuna, Poland	219.9
1976	Karl Schnabl, Austria	234.8

NORDIC SKIING (continued)

WOMEN'S 5-KM CROSS-COUNTRY

		MIN.-SEC.
1964	Claudia Boyarskikh, U.S.S.R.	17:50.5
1968	Toini Gustafsson, Sweden	16:45.2
1972	Galina Koulakova, U.S.S.R.	17:00.50
1976	Helena Takalo, Finland	15:48.69

WOMEN'S 10-KM CROSS-COUNTRY

		MIN.-SEC.
1952	Lydia Wideman, Finland	41:40.0
1956	Lyubov Kosyreva, U.S.S.R.	38:11.0
1960	Mariya Gusakova, U.S.S.R.	39:46.6
1964	Claudia Boyarskikh, U.S.S.R.	40:24.3
1968	Toini Gustafsson, Sweden	36:46.5
1972	Galina Koulakova, U.S.S.R.	34:17.82
1976	Raisa Smetanina, U.S.S.R.	30:13.41

WOMEN'S 15-KM CROSS-COUNTRY RELAY

		HR.-MIN.-SEC.
1956	Finland	1:09:01.0
1960	Sweden	1:04:21.4
1964	U.S.S.R.	59:20.2
1968	Norway	57:30.0
1972	U.S.S.R.	48:46.15
1976	U.S.S.R.	1:07:49.75*

*20 km

SPEED SKATING

MEN'S 500 M

		SEC.
1924	Charles Jewtraw, U.S.	44.0
1928	Tie between	
	Clas Thunberg, Finland, and	
	Bernt Evensen, Norway	43.4
1932	John Shea, U.S.	43.4
1936	Ivar Ballangrud, Norway	43.4
1948	Finn Helgesen, Norway	43.1
1952	Ken Henry, U.S.	43.2
1956	Yevgeni Grishin, U.S.S.R.	40.2
1960	Yevgeni Grishni, U.S.S.R.	40.2
1964	Terry McDermott, U.S.	40.1
1968	Erhard Keller, West Germany	40.3
1972	Erhard Keller, West Germany	39.44
1976	Yevgeni Kulikov, U.S.S.R.	39.17

MEN'S 1,000 M

		MIN.-SEC.
1976	Peter Mueller, U.S.	1:19.32

MEN'S 1,500 M

		MIN.-SEC.
1924	Clas Thunberg, Finland	2:20.8
1928	Clas Thunberg, Finland	2:21.1
1932	John Shea, U.S.	2:57.5
1936	Charles Mathisen, Norway	2:19.2
1948	Sverre Farstad, Norway	2:17.6
1952	Hjalmar Andersen, Norway	2:20.4
1956	Tie between	
	Yuri Mikhailov and	
	Yevgeni Grishin, U.S.S.R.	2:08.6
1960	Tie between	
	Roald Edgar Aas, Norway, and	
	Yevgeni Grishin, U.S.S.R.	2:10.4
1964	Ants Antson, U.S.S.R.	2:10.3
1968	Kees Verkerk, Netherlancs	2:03.4
1972	Ard Schenk, Netherlands	2:02.96
1976	Jan Egil Storholt, Norway	1:59.38

SPEED SKATING
(continued)

MEN'S 5,000 M

		MIN.-SEC.
1924	Clas Thunberg, Finland	8:39.0
1928	Ivar Ballangrud, Norway	8:50.5
1932	Irving Jaffee, U.S.	9:40.8
1936	Ivar Ballangrud, Norway	8:19.6
1948	Reidar Liaklev, Norway	8:29.4
1952	Hjalmar Andersen, Norway	8:10.6
1956	Boris Shilkov, U.S.S.R.	7:48.7
1960	Viktor Kosichkin, U.S.S.R.	7:51.3
1964	Knut Johannesen, Norway	7:38.4
1968	Fred Anton Maier, Norway	7:22.4
1972	Ard Schenk, Netherlands	7:23.61
1976	Sten Stensen, Norway	7:24.48

MEN'S 10,000 M

		MIN.-SEC.
1924	Julien Skutnabb, Finland	18:04.8
1928	No contest because ice thawed.	
1932	Irving Jaffee, U.S.	19:13.6
1936	Ivar Ballangrud, Norway	17:24.3
1948	Ake Seyffarth, Norway	17:26.3
1952	Hjalmar Andersen, Norway	16:45.8
1956	Sigvard Ericsson, Sweden	16:35.9
1960	Knut Johannesen, Norway	15:46.6
1964	Jonny Nilsson, Sweden	15:50.1
1968	Johnny Hoeglin, Sweden	15:23.6
1972	Ard Schenk, Netherlands	15:01.35
1976	Piet Kleine, Netherlands	14:50.59

SPEED SKATING
(continued)

WOMEN'S 500 M

		SEC.
1960	Helga Haase, Germany	45.9
1964	Lidia Skoblikova, U.S.S.R.	45.0
1968	Ludmilla Titova, U.S.S.R.	46.1
1972	Anne Henning, U.S.	43.33
1976	Sheila Young, U.S.	42.76

WOMEN'S 1,000 M

		MIN.-SEC.
1960	Klara Guseva, U.S.S.R.	1:34.1
1964	Lidia Skoblikova, U.S.S.R.	1:33.2
1968	Carolina Geijssen, Netherlands	1:32.6
1972	Monika Pflug, West Germany	1:31.40
1976	Tatyana Averina, U.S.S.R.	1:28.43

WOMEN'S 1,500 M

		MIN.-SEC.
1960	Lidia Skoblikova, U.S.S.R.	2:25.2
1964	Lidia Skoblikova, U.S.S.R.	2:22.6
1968	Kaija Mustonen, Finland	2:22.4
1972	Dianne Holum, U.S.	2:20.85
1976	Galina Stepanskaya, U.S.S.R.	2:16.58

WOMEN'S 3,000 M

		MIN.-SEC.
1960	Lidia Skoblikova, U.S.S.R.	5:14.3
1964	Lidia Skoblikova, U.S.S.R.	5:14.9
1968	Johanna Schut, Netherlands	4:56.2
1972	Stien Baas-Kaiser, Netherlands	4:52.14
1976	Tatyana Averina, U.S.S.R.	4:45.19

Other Books on the Olympics

There are few good books on the Winter Olympics. The best is the *Encyclopedia of the Winter Olympics,* by Erich Kamper, published in 1964 in West Germany by Union Verlag Stuttgärt. It contains extensive descriptions of each Winter Olympics through 1960, with names of all competitors and an alphabetical list of all medalists. The same text appears in English, German, French and Swedish. The major shortcoming is that there is no material from 1964 on.

The Story of the Olympic Games, 776 B.C. to 1976, by John Kieran, Arthur Daley and Pat Jordan, contains chapters on each set of summer games through 1976. From 1948 on, the Winter Olympics get good but limited coverage. J. B. Lippincott Co. publishes an updated edition every four years.

The United States Olympic Committee publishes a large book every four years with extensive reports on the most recent summer and winter games. Information on these books is available from the United States Olympic Committee, 1750 East Boulder Street, Colorado Springs, Colorado, U.S.A. 80909.

Index